Directionally Challenged
(but finding my way home)

By

Susan J. Mitchell

Dedicated to my son Reuben, the most important person in my world; I admire you and respect the challenges you have faced with so much more courage than I ever could.
I am so glad you are my son.

OLD SEVENTY CREEK PRESS

COPYRIGHT 2014 BY Susan J. Mitchell

2014 OLD SEVENTY CREEK PRESS FIRST EDITION

PRINTED IN THE UNITED STATES OF AMERICA
ALL RIGHTS RESERVED UNDER INTERNATIONAL
AND PAN-AMERICAN COPYRIGHT CONVENTIONS
PUBLISHED IN THE UNITED STATES
BY OLD SEVENTY CREEK PRESS

RUDY THOMAS, PUBLISHER
P. O. BOX 204
ALBANY, KENTUCKY 42602

ISBN-13: 978-0615936369 (Old Seventy Creek Press)

ISBN-10: 0615936369

Cover photo by Susan J. Mitchell, all rights reserved...

Table of Contents

Sunrise

As the sun pushes its way out
of the remnants of yesterday,
I reach out from under blankets of sleep,
risking the burn of day,
to shove it back into darkness.
My reach is not long enough and
I retrieve a hand full of clouds instead.

I suppose I should be grateful I can touch them,
but right now I am just not ready
for the morning to begin.
I heard the crack of dawn
and it sounded like a sonic boom
that even the strongest coffee
could not quiet.

It ripped its way into the night
laughing hysterically
at the stars' surprise
and spilled crimson and orange
on the silken darkness.

I smelled morning
with its drops of dew
and untouched grass
then I stretched and rose
and wiped the clouds
from my fingers

This Secret Lover

I try to become the writer I need to be
as I look for jobs by day
but sneak away in the night to my
glorious hideaway filled with words.

I hear them whisper underneath
the cover of the wind.
I must entice them to my notebook
before they are carried
                                        beyond my reach.

I lay down in emotion
                        thick as mud
and hope, before dawn,
            I have washed away the evidence
                        onto scraps of paper.

It's as though I have taken
a secret lover –
            and I have –
because these words understand me
before I comprehend them.

They make me cry
long before they reach the page
and again when they do.
It's love that goes beyond

love making.

It's these conversations that
    lure my soul
        until I weep,
not from sadness
  but from the beauty I experienced
    without knowing
        it existed
    and the realization
           the beauty came
             from inside
                me.

Warm Breeze

Love blew in my window today.
It came on a summer breeze
like a wish drifting from
a blown out birthday candle.
It brushed my skin
      as it passed by –
            a stranger on a subway
            with somewhere else to go.
I looked out the window to see
from whence it came.

Was it from the young mother
playing tag with her son in the park
or the man mowing his elderly neighbor's lawn?
Could it have come from the girl on the bench
writing an apology for her misspoken words?

Maybe it was a thought
sent out into the universe
from the other side of the world
and carried to me on a series
of winds.

I could not tell the direction
or the mileage
only that I was touched
and warmed by its presence.

So I searched for someone
whose presence warmed me
and whispered, "I am glad
you are here."

The wind picked up my words
to carry them to someone else
who had an open window.

Trust

Trust tastes like a song
on my tongue for the first time
before I even know the words.

Trust smells like a receiving
blanket the color of the ocean
when the sun hits it just right.

Trust feels like a summer rock
above the river where we left our towels
and our shoes before we jumped.

Trust looks like an oak tree in autumn,
its leaves on the ground, branches outstretched
knowing it will be naked for months.

When Next the Dew Falls*

Come, come see the dew,
this sodden forgiveness of yesterday,
nature's way of cleansing the palate
of the flavor of a day already
an aftertaste. Feel drops that fell in the darkness,
like a mother's goodnight kisses telling
you the world and your place in it is
exactly as it should be. Let your gaze
skim, like rocks to the river, across
these diamonds on leaves, grass, the tire swing
dangling from the oak branch. As sunrise pours
across an emerging horizon, experience the thirst
to resume your voyage to discover who you
are and who you will be when next
the dew falls.

*First published in Motif Volume 2: Come What May (Motes Books, 2010)

Talking to the Night

Night fell.
Actually, it tripped over dusk
and landed hard
right in my front yard,
too embarrassed to get up.

So, we talked --
night laying there
hands behind its head
looking up at the stars.
I sat on the porch swing
gently guided by
a whisper from the universe.

Our words floated like motes
under a bright light.
They swayed like bees
waltzing among flowers.

Our pauses were quiet
like a campfire,
patient like a mare
watching her foal stand
the first time.

We laughed.
The laughter of Night

was the sound of wind
whistling beside the house
as the world sleeps.
It was the vision of fireflies
lighting the world one
flash at a time.

Then Night stood up,
dusted dirt from midnight robes,
thanked me for my time
and with a wave as grateful
as an early morning cloud,
disappeared into a crimson dawn.

Horizons

Friendship is abstract
as a dawn horizon.

The sky and tree tops
meet in the distance
and embrace
as only Mother Nature
would have it.

Yet the exact place
where the two connect
is elusive.
No one can reach out
and touch the two
at once.
Though they appear as
one continuous picture.

But they are
separate as two individuals.

One must remain rooted
to the ground
While the other
rises above
The world.
One is light

while the other gives air.

Although there is no proof they
are connected at all,
the sky and the tree tops,
no doubt,
forever feel the other's presence

and both are more beautiful
because of it.

I Touched a Shadow Today

I touched a shadow today.
Just stretched out one hand
and my fingertips feathered across
its silky texture.

It looked at me –
stared right into my eyes
as if touched for the first time

Then turned to walk beside me,
hands behind its back,
gazing about as if on its
maiden voyage of my evening walk.

We drifted quietly so as not
to disturb the moment.
The sun lay down before us
on a citrus horizon.

I turned to retrace my steps
back to the comfort of my porch.
Our eyes met again. The shadow reached
toward me and, with the warmth
of a Summer breeze, hugged me close
then disappeared
as silent as a setting sun.

Hell's Winter

The snow was of no
consequence

It was the cold,
the frozen air that seeped
through my pores,
finding its way under
my rib cage to swirl
among my innards
leaving me with frostbitten
organs that might never
be warm again

this, this winter that has lasted
into a new decade
and laughs at blooming dogwoods
as their flowers retreat
into themselves then fall, shivering
to the ground must have been
blasted by a blue breeze
hurled from a hell frozen over.

This Thing She Found

It was bigger than life
this thing she found.

It was in the shower
but could not be washed away.

It reminded her of her mother,
her grandmother, her daughter,
the granddaughter she did not yet have.

It reminded her of what she was meant to do
and what she had not done.

This little thing she could not actually see
made her look at her life, her friends, her family

without judgment, without pettiness,
but filled with love and fear.

She stood there in a moment,
for a lifetime.

She wanted to show someone, no one.

She felt the water flow over her, all of her
and yet she felt nothing.

Was the water hot, cold?
Was she still standing there?

She had somehow moved through time,
saw her life crawl in front of her.
There was no flash to it.

She looked at the years and wondered
where she had been this whole time.

She had found it, but how did it get there?
How long before there would be nothing in its place?

Who should she tell first, last?
Her body was heavy, her thoughts jumbled.

This tiny thing no one could possibly see
was there as sure as she was.
Its importance and its insignificance
somehow identical.

Even if it was nothing, it was something and
she would never be the same.

She had found a lump.

After the Lump

I poured onto the couch --
a body filled to the toenails
with exhaustion and
enough left over to sit on my chest
mocking the fact that I have
done nothing to physically warrant
such a consequence.

You have.

I merely waited while the doctor carved
from you an arrogant obstruction that grew
of its own free will, not caring
that it did not belong
and was of no usefulness to your life.

I took you home then rushed to the pharmacy
to purchase pain meds before the demon unleashed
itself upon you like a heavy shadow that smothered
your every breath.
But I was too late. It was within you
before I could return.
Shiny red bandages lay in the trash,
fear was on your face and in your eyes.

We returned to the place of knives and healing
and I watched as they replaced

your new bandages with newer, whiter ones.
I heard you cry out in pain.
I observed your heartbeat
slow to a level barely above coding
on the machines attached to you.

Your eyes looked at me,
but it was as if we were too far apart.
You blurred before me.
I was in a fog before you.
We were losing our grip:
you to the pain from the thing that was removed,
me to the thing that seemed to be taking you.

The night was filled with beeping sounds
and apparitions wearing scrubs entering
and exiting at all hours.
There was nothing either of us could do.
We were at the mercy of those who touched you.
Your voice was distant, faint.
Your will strong.
Your eyes heavy.

I was lost in the midst of questions
and the fear of Divine Intervention.
Finally, it was just us in the night-filled room.
Dawn came slowly, hesitantly
as if unsure what her light might reveal.
A shift change brought new and improved apparitions.

They smiled, poked, prodded,
monitored the beeping.

A doctor emerged, examined
the hole that was left,
said you were free to go home
and evaporated into the mist.
You smiled.
Today your eyes were clear.

Together we packed up your things.
Your movements slow, cautious.
I signed papers, brought the car
to the door and watched someone
wheel you toward me,

My eyes as happy to see you then
as if we had been apart for a lifetime.

Human Tornado

There is no air. The grass stands tall, knowing what
 is coming. The animals have gone to their homes
     and do not even speak, lest the wind hear them.
      How does everyone, but me, understand and
      acknowledge what Mother Nature is about
       to do? Why do I fight the characteristics
   of people and ignore human nature as
   it wreaks misery on my life while the
       rest of the world watches as if it is
     a movie worthy of popcorn and
     candy? I see the sky turn green
  and marvel at its beauty. The
    neighbors are heading for
    shelter in their basement.
 They look over their
shoulders right
 before they
   disappear.
      Now it's just you &
        me.

Cinnamon Swirl Women

We walk to the bakery
to buy cinnamon swirl bread

Discussing
how women are shoved
into situations where they are
forced to allow men to publicly touch them
       --unwanted hugs,
         a kiss on the cheek —

Like bread into
a toaster without its consent,
heated to a golden crisp,
tossed onto a plate
and buttered to add flavor.

We wonder who told them we were
their breakfast.

Friend

Drip your colors onto
          paper and swirl them around
     into words so I can see
         the brush strokes of your life.
I cannot find you in the shadows of
         grays and blacks and muted sounds
     that breathe in the night.
Pour your paint, no matter how
         drab or brilliant,
     don't hide the shades
     you think are ugly, let me
see your world in all its shrill and
         violent smudges and mistakes.
         Let me admire the misspoken
     words and the ill-fated, misshapen
         faces and the disfigured
          songs you sing alone
when no one else can hear.
         Give me the parts of you
that spiral out of control
     without reason and I will
show you the beauty in chaos
         and tell you again
     how much I love you.

Thoughts of You

Thoughts
          of you

are like a blanket
          and pillow

in the corner
          of a room

next to my favorite
          book shelf,

waiting to wrap around
me and let me lay my

          head down
while I read a story

that carries us
                    away

to places where we
play like children

and marvel at the
          world

that brought us
                    together

in the first place.

New Life

I am ready for a new life. There is
no baby on the way, no wedding bells, no
       new job or new location.
Just a new mindset, new demeanor.
I am shedding my old skin for one that fits
me better. There is a conscious sweeping up
of old shadows and words, of old thoughts and
beliefs, mostly about myself and my abilities.

I have found new paths around old walls that, before,
brought me to a standstill. The cold does not scare me,
the fog does not intimidate me. It is okay if I do not do
everything right. I look forward to wrong turns,
knowing they are an indication that I continue on my way.
Being directionally challenged is not a hindrance,
but a guarantee I will see more of the world than I intended.

I am ready to stand up and let the world know I am present.
I am here and I belong.
When I stumble over wrong choices, I will understand
that my stumble is not a complete stop.
A few bruises here and there will not mean I have failed,
but that I have found a new way that something was not
       successful.
It will not mean I am not successful.
It will ensure that I am continuing to prove that I am ready
for my new life.

Home Cooking

I watch like a sponge lying
on the ocean floor,
absorbing the world washing
over, around and through me.

I see the two of them,
husband and wife,
synchronized swimmers –
a consenting aquatic couple
always aware of the other's
presence.

They are different breeds of fish
with complimentary colors
and similar tastes.

They live in a home where Jesus
comes to dinner. He sips coffee
beside her, puts His hand on her
shoulder as she speaks.

Sands of kindness, love and respect
massage guests' bare feet
and lodge deep in the hair of a
puppy who begs to play fetch.

Life's ripples are solved by riding
Waves to find the cause
then digested with Saturday's
homemade blueberry pancakes
and put to rest during a long
family nap.

It is full immersion into a relationship
not everyone has to understand
because it does not matter
who flips the pancakes or
who feeds the dog
                    just that no one goes hungry.

Gold Fish

There you are
in your glass, aquatic home

Staring at me
as if I have something of yours.

When I come closer
you dart the other direction

Pretending you were not watching
and that I cannot see you.

You swim around your world
with the memory of a gnat

Not knowing that five minutes ago
was not yesterday

And next week
does not begin in an hour.

When someone leaves
you do not know it was not supposed to happen

The time spent grieving is miniscule
especially if it happens at feeding time

when manna drops from the sky
and fills your world with riches beyond belief.

Some days I wish I lived
underwater in a city of plastic vegetation

and colorful rocks
where all you have to do to know you are alive

is breathe
and watch the air bubbles rise.

Both Sides of Town

Blue lights flash from police cars.
Officers lead the neighbor's boyfriend, handcuffed,
to a waiting cruiser, help him sit comfortably
in the back seat, then drive to the place
where he will sleep at night and get three meals a day.
The boyfriend will brag to his cellmates
about his escapades and lament his treatment
by everyone who has come in contact with him
since before he was first awarded the silver bracelets.

Back at the neighbor's apartment the search continues.
Drawers are opened, closets pilfered.
private things are touched.
Pills are found, but they belong to someone else, the
girlfriend tells the officers.
No, that money is what she had saved from her
near-minimum wage job. No, she did not know
he was selling to people who came to the apartment.

Then the tears came. Yes, she knew.
She tried to get him to stop. She thought
he had. He promised.

Across town, red lights flash from an ambulance.
Pills spilled on the floor next to the bed
are crushed under the wheels of the stretcher
as an unconscious teenager is heaved upon it.

A mother looks frantically for her keys
as she still holds in her hand the phone from
which she had called 911.

As the boyfriend changes into his orange jump suit
and gets his picture taken,

      As the neighbor dries her eyes and shows
      where her boyfriend kept his inventory,

As the mother finds her keys, rushes to the hospital and is
told to sit in the waiting area,

The emergency room doctor is noting the time of death.

Getting Clean

I lay across the floor
scrubbing dirt only I can see,
so close to my face
I cannot miss it.
Dirt, like the drugs filling my son's
body, filling in the memory
lapses like blackness in grout.

I scrub until the bristles ache
like my heart when I wiped
the liquid charcoal from his lips.

He asks the same question
over and over again,
the same one I ask the floor
as I stare at the suds and puddles,
"How did I get here?"

We were together most of his
life. The two of us.
we played in the park,
ate ice cream.
I gave him his first puppy.
He named the mutt, Tony.
I never knew why.

Now I smell the lemon-fresh
scent of my kitchen floor,
counters, mirrors, sink,
shower, toilet.
How did I get here?

I remember watching him
as he unfastened his seat belt
to get out of the car
and walk into school by himself,
knowing someday he would walk
into places I had not taken him.
I never imagined it would be
this place.

I dip the brush deep into the bucket
as if answers had settled to the bottom.
Steam rises as smoke from a bong
in a room filled with people
I would never invite to my home;
I tell my son his black tongue
reminds me of our dog, Sam,
with the purple tongue.
"How did I get here?" he asks.

We used to walk across the huge
lawn of a nearby church every Friday
on our way to pick up a pizza.
In the dusk he ran ahead and

lay down in the grass, "Mommy,
can you find me?"
I always did.

I hold the Styrofoam cup so
he can drink more of the liquid
designed to save a life.
He looks at me with eyes that
shake too much for him to
see me and I cannot find him.
How did we get here?

My kitchen floor has puddles
as if the rain had come in,
a muddy, dirty rain.

I dip the mop in fresh, clear
water, twist it until the excess
runs back where it came from.
I envision my son's dealer,
my hands wrapped around
his throat
       twisting, twisting.

I clean up the water,
empty the bucket,
lay on the couch.
The floor will dry on its own.
We all need time to dry out.

After Your Indiscretion

Lay naked across the bed like
   Sunset on the horizon.
      I will admire your beauty
One inch at a time.
   Only this time
      Say the words as though I have
Never heard them fall from your
   Lips until now.
      One soft syllable at a time.
Envelope me in a moment
   I seem to have
      Lost since
Last we were together. When you
   Told me how my eyes drank you in
      As if you were a fine wine.
Instill in me the brief but
   Unforgiveable feeling of
      Trust. Will to me that
Negotiable emotion of love. Wrap me in
   Delicate lies that caress my skin like poison
      Ivy on a summer's day. Stroke
Every part of my soul as you did before: imagining someone
   Else much more deserving that I. But for
      Once let me gaze at up. Let me watch as your
Skin peels from your body and see how your colors change
      Now that I know who you are and
Still cannot force myself to leave.

Swept Up

I want to throw things across the room
and watch the glorious destruction
of our relationship

as our conversations slam against walls
shattering words into syllables
that no longer make sense or ring true.

I want to feel the shards
of splintered promises as they
slither beneath my skin
spewing blood that
runs like you have,

making me weak from
forgiving over and over
when it no longer made sense.

I want you to break
and fall to the floor
in pieces that cannot be mended

until I have to sweep you up
with the dirt and dust and grime
and hear the joyous twinkling
like glass exploding in a kitchen sink.

I want to hear the words you have
hurled at me though your mind
and barely caught before
they reached your tongue.

Share with me the body blows
and the right hook
I heard in your voice.

Dare me, then double dare me
to tell you
I still love you

as we lay crumpled on the floor
among silences and sobs
that never let us say
what we really meant.

Missed Opportunities

Come away with me, you say.
Let's find out what
we have and have not.
Let's touch with our eyes,
our hearts and see
if our souls are moved.

Wait, I say,
are we the right color,
the right age, the right gender?
What if our souls are moved
and we realize what
we have we should not?

Come stay with me, you say.
Let's hide away in a world
of two where nature is
our home and the trees our judge.
Let's see if the streams
quench our thirst and the mountain
air allows us to breathe.

Wait, I say.
Are we ready? Are we prepared
to defend ourselves from what lies
in the darkness? Will we drown
in the water that quenches us?

Come sit with me, you say.
We will listen to the silence
and hear our story told
by the wind and our sighs.

Wait, I say.
What if someone hears us?
Our story will take wind
and grow in size. What if
they do not understand?

Wait here, you say.
I hear your footsteps fading
in the distance.

Come back, I say. I am ready.

Coffee Mug Identity

Sunlight pours through the
window, drips onto my closed
eye lids and runs down my face.

I set the alarm for late morning
but wake two and a half hours before.

Fluttering early day sounds
caress my open ears.
My body floats on the bed as if on water.

Awake, I dream of what I could
have been, what my life was
supposed to be by now.

When the alarm screams its
warning, I rise as mist on water
and walk to the kitchen to find
out who I am.

I taste the umber liquid the coffee maker
spills out and realize again why
I rarely drink it:
it's not me.

This container I live in
houses my things, provides a place

to sleep but gives no hint of my identity.
Who is this middle aged woman
who once had a home, a family,
those societal measures of success?

I sip coffee from an earthen mug
that will hold anything
I pour into it

not because it is mine
but because that is what
it was meant to do.

Saturday

I lay here on this Saturday morning
that brushes past me
like someone in a hurry.

The hushed day before
light creeps in
sounds like when he lay beside me
and breathed a dream
that caused him to turn over
and brush my skin with sleepy fingertips.

His eyes might open
to see if I was real.
Other times, he knew.
He knew.

Lost Honesty

What if Honesty
did more than lay between us
untouched?

What if it stood up,
walked over and sat
in the space where
words had been?

Would you look at me
and would I understand?
If it came close enough
to touch us
could we breathe it in
and let it out
alongside forgiveness?

There must be something
simpler than this web
we are in.
Maybe if we just sat
closer and remembered
who we are
we could try again.

Our Ichthus

This path we have traveled
has crisscrossed in ways
we did not imagine

The shape of an ichthus
with that spiritual feeling
of having been in the right place
with the right person
for the right amount of time

Now we are going
different directions
because that is the nature
of the design

This does not mean
our time together is over

Our drawing is not finished,
just more complete
because of where we have been.

Edge

I close my eyes
and, like a balloon,
I float precariously
near the edge.
All it would take
for me
to fall off
is a gust of wind
from a butterfly's wings.

Roughage

I heard it coming,
this tornado.
It sounded just like it was supposed to:
      like a train.
When it hit,
there was nothing I could do
but be tossed like
lettuce in the salad of life.

Yesterday is Closed

At midnight, Yesterday closed and locked its door
as I pushed hard against it, looking out into
a dawn dripping of Today. I was not prepared
to see the citrus colored sunlight
spilled on the horizon like a breakfast drink
on This Morning's paper.

Sticky words on the news at hand
remind me why I want to return to the darkness
and not surface until I have skipped over Today
like a rock bouncing across a lake's surface
into Tomorrow or Next Week or whenever we are
okay and life is calm and comforting again.

Our Dance

Your words are like distant drums
from a native tribe
       war music
that I have come to know

only I did not know how
to stop the rhythm
to change the music
to make this dance
       New

I do not want to apply
paint to our faces
our bodies
to listen to the
escalating beat as our
       words pound each other
  with hurt and accusation
from years of togetherness
and knowing
our faults both imagined and real

I want to change
the rhythm from battlefield
weaponry and language
of bombs and bullets

I want the instrument
to stop being pain and retaliation

Tomorrow when I hear
a rumble of drums introducing
the oncoming battle that is sure
          to consume us

I will hum to myself
music that will sweep
me toward a more promising
          Dance

In my head will play –
          not a song of war
                    but one that will offer steps
toward peace and happiness –
I will hear   the Rumba.

Conversation with My Soul

My soul came of age
and floated along the breeze
through years of trees
and birds and natural things.

Then, tired, she lay down in dirt
black as Kentucky coal,
warm as breakfast coffee.
She dug deep
and drank long
until her body rose up
and walked away.

To find a place in the world
where richness and darkness
were valued as something akin
to spirituality and knowing.

She continues on her path.
Sometimes she stops by
to sit quietly at the table,
two steaming cups between us.

After a while, I look her direction
and she is gone.
Her presence remains
as a comfort.

I rinse the dishes,
dry my hands.

Someday she will
find the answers
among the other souls
she meets along the way

and she will return
with a conversation
worth the wait.

Creek, Wind and Soul

Creek,
play me the music
that makes you weep.

Sparrow,
sing me the song
that makes you think.

Geese,
tell me the story
that takes you places.

Fish,
show me what you learned
that makes you thirst for more.

Wind,
whisper to me the words
that take your breath away.

Fire,
color the night with a picture
of what ignites you.

Snow,
help me feel that which sends
shivers down your spine.

Tornado,
look me in the eye so I can see
what moves you.

Soul,
tell me
what gives you life.

Something Spiritual

Live a life
as true as poetry,
as beautiful as a
living sunrise.

Dream until you
find the purpose
of your soul,
then paint the world
your favorite color.

In the quiet of a
listening heart
is the possibility
of a life
we were meant
to live.

Photograph

At the nursing home's Christmas party
they took her picture with Santa helping
her open the package.

The photo did not show
what was inside the box,
but her eyes were bright as a child's
as she peered into the box covered
in, now torn, red paper.

She was like any other
woman trapped in a wheelchair,
locked in a mind that would not remember
breakfast or family.

But in that moment,
at that second,
in a day of many seconds,
she was,
while the flash filled her excited face,
she was,
      forever,
         Grandma.

Soul for Sale

He said he had sold his soul
and I wondered how many coins
he had earned.

My own soul, content
in her home, though always interested
in wandering, I could not imagine
would go if I sold her.

How would I get her to leave
with her purchaser?
She clings to me, not out of fear,
but because she belongs not *to* me
                                    with me.

Why would I sell her?
She, who inspires me with ideas of her own.
She, who takes care of me by painting
me with colors only the two of us can see
and I alone can feel.

She swirls inside me with brushes and wings
fluttering paint into a design all her own
that becomes me or I become it
without knowing I have changed in the slightest.

He said he had sold his soul.

What had it come to
that life demanded payment
and his soul was up for auction?
What color will he be
when there are no brushes left inside him,
no wisps of wings,
no palette filled with dabs of acrylic or oils
waiting to be swirled into a design
he had not known
          was being created
by the only one who knew him
                    well enough to know
he had not gotten a fair price?

How to Drive Home

Warm up the car.
It has gotten a lot colder since
you parked it before the Super Bowl
came on the television.
Scrape the ice from the windows
then go get your 4-year-old son
and fasten him in the car seat.

Back slowly out of the driveway
and pull up to the stop sign.
Look at your son and pat his leg.
He will be the last person you
see with both your eyes.
You will be the last person
to touch his femur before it snaps.

Turn left onto the deserted rural
road. After you pass through town,
go around the right hand curve,
let your front wheels touch
the black ice that slings you into
the other lane.

Hit fully, directly and unintentionally
the car coming toward you.
Don't worry, you won't see them completely cover
the other driver with the blanket.

You will be unbuckling your seat
belt and reaching for your
screaming son before
all goes black and you
don't arrive home until Spring.

When I am a Painting

We often say
    when I grow up …
        and hope we never do

if I believed I could be
    anything I want to be
        then I would say …

when I am a child
    I will be precocious
        and happy

when I am a painting
    I will be colorful
        and vibrant

when I am a poem
    I will be thoughtful
        and remembered

when I am a color
    I will be deep
        and beautiful

when I am a sun beam
    I will be warm
        and bright

if I believed I could be
            anything,

I would know
                    I could be all of this

when I grow up.

Landlord, Could You Fix This?

Landlord,
could you fix the leak in the shower
the one that drips, drips … drips
at night like ancient torture?

Landlord,
could you fix the roof
so I can hear the rain
dance a rhythm across
the rafters
then roll into the gutters
and drain into downspouts
as if running off stage
when the curtain falls?

Landlord,
could you fix the walls
so I can hear the neighbor
whisper *I love you* to his wife
but cannot hear him
push her against our adjoining wall until she
knocks my pictures off their hooks
and books off my shelf?

Landlord,
could you fix the creak in the floor
so the tenants below

cannot hear me on Fridays
when I wiggle and jiggle and shake off
the week of my life I sold to a company
of thieves who believe they own my very breath?

Landlord,
could you fix the windows
so they lure warm breezes inside
to wipe away winter and freshen
the air with sounds of birds
and the promise of Spring?

Landlord,
could you fix the refrigerator
so it will hold enough food for me
and the child next door who cries at night
after all the money was spent on
magical white powder for his parents
and none on milk or bread?

Landlord,
could you wait a bit longer for my rent?
I need to pay my utilities and keep the lights on
so I can read the classifieds.
'Cause, you see, I was laid off today.

Pieces of Us

Burrow with me
under handmade quilts
made by our grandmothers and aunts.
By flashlight I will
read you my poetry
so the words can fall on a pillow top
mattress while we hide under our
ancestor's patchwork stories.

Don't say a word when I am done.
Let me look at your face,
your eyes and I will know
if the stanzas moved you
as I intended.

Then we will push the poems aside,
listening to what was sewn
into our history by the women
keeping us warm.

Body Language

Sleep teased my eye lids,
deepened my breath.
Here in this spoon of us

I was with the one I loved
  I knew beyond the shadows
    of slumber that
if I reached out of my dream
  I could touch the core of you

My fingertips traced a thought
  as the world beyond
  grew quiet and hushed
you held your breath and listened
as my touch whispered
  that we were alone
  and I loved you now
more than I had ever loved
    another human being
      in my life

Memory

Memory evaporates as
morning fog in the yard.
Seems like the fog lasts longer
out in the field.

Thoughts are catch as
catch can,
like water through a colander
       only bits of it stay inside.

As I get older
the fogs and the bits will intertwine
and create a world that may or may not
have ever existed.

I will believe I am in a time
when my family is young and my son,
a grown man now, is a precocious child.

"We have to get ready to go to the zoo," I will
explain to him. "We are going to ride
the camel and listen to a man talk about eagles"

As if I have special powers to see
ahead of time
what we will do
when, in reality,

All of this is in the past
and I will think
it has not yet happened.

       How precious it will be
       to believe we can
       live our life over again,
       knowing the outcome
       before we begin.

Lines in the Sand

There was a line in the sand
that they did not draw
but dared not cross

What would it matter if they did?

At night the ocean comes closer, closer
swishing away the line with every wave
until in the morning the beach is naked

except for new seashells,
            carcasses of the unlucky crustaceans
            who gave up their lives for tourists

soon people would gather
with sticks and draw more lines
for others not to cross

like magic or politics
            people stayed on their own side of the line
            watching the others just out of their reach

living amazing lives

            until night came and the tide sneaked in
erasing borders no one understood

Fifteen Grandchildren

She tells the young agent on the phone that she has
fifteen grandchildren
scattered across the country.
They have good jobs and are
starting their own families.
Her children are too far away
to visit often so she calls
this nice gentleman
to help her figure out
how to pay for
this nursing home where she lives.

      His computer screen stares at him,
      wide-eyed and unblinking.

On good days her arthritis
really isn't so bad.
Her hip hurts sometimes
but not the one she had replaced.
That one is doing much better.

      He jumps from screen to screen
      like an acrobat in the circus.

May I put you on hold?
Yes, honey, take your time.
I have all day.

His supervisor says she will have to pay
for everything herself
        from her fixed income
                that is less per month
        than half the cost
        of the nursing home.
        She will have to sell the house
        her late husband built for her
        when they first married.

Thank you for holding.
Honey, that's okay. Did I
tell you I have fifteen grandchildren?

She's met some nice people there.
The man across the hall
doesn't get out of his room much
since they changed his medication.

                The computer gives the agent words
                he is required to read
                that tells this woman
                with a voice like his own Grandma
                there is no help for her here.

The food is good and
if she doesn't feel well
they will bring it right to
her room and help her with it

if there is enough staff working.

What? The insurance won't pay?
Oh, dear.

His computer screen stares at him,
mocking, unflinching.
Each screen
repeating, confirming
there is no help here.

Well, honey, you've done
All you can do –
Her voice cracks.
Thank you for your help.

She slowly lays the phone
in its cradle.
The connection is severed.
The line goes dead.

He pushes the 'not ready' button
on his phone, put his head in his hands,
closes his eyes.

He tries not to remember
she has fifteen grandchildren.

He takes a few deep breaths,

pushes the 'ready' button.
His headset beeps.
"Thank you for calling Medicare.
How may I help you?"

Gone Fishing

for Frankie

I wish I had taken him fishing
that day. After all, I had taken
him the first time. I wish
I could have taken him *that* day.
Maybe the outcome would
have been different.
He did not want to leave
but his friends did, so, with
great reluctance and frustration,
he put away his pole and folded
his tall, lanky body into
the back seat, strapped himself in.

I wish I had taken him fishing
that day. After all, I had taken
him the first time.

My nephew had called
me when he was seven years old and
begged me to take him fishing until I
said yes. I knew nothing about fishing except
that fish lived in water and
you need a pole and bait to get
them to bite.

So, I went to the store
where people knew about such things.
A woman taught me how to cast
until we caught an unsuspecting
customer. Then she taught me
to put wiggly, squiggly worms
on a sharp hook because
fish, for some reason, will not
bite unless they see food.

One sunny day after school,
I picked him up in my new
car. It was just the two of us.
He was wiggly, squiggly
with excitement.
We took our poles and bait,
walked onto the pier
of an empty lake.
He listened to my instructions
as if my words would
someday save his life.
I wish they could have.

We sat quietly listening to
the wind brushing the lake water
and tussling the leaves of the trees.
He clicked his tennis shoes together
as he waited for a fish to bite.   After awhile
he asked what I too was wondering,

"Why aren't we catching any fish?"
"I don't know," I tell him.
I had the attention span of
a seven year old myself that day
so when he said he had
fished enough, I was ready
to go, too. It was a
mutual agreement, not one
made for him by friends not interested
in what he wanted. They should
have listened to him that day.

As we walked to the car
his only disappointment was
slipping on lake slime and falling
in. His mother had warned him
not to get my car dirty.
So, we covered the seat with
a blanket and fastened his seat
belt. He smiled all the way home.
We had not caught a single fish
but we did drown a few worms
and became connected to each other
with fishing line that could
sever the fingers of anyone who
tried to break it.
I was glad I had taken him
fishing that day.

But on that *other* day, the one
on which I wished I had taken him
fishing, he did not fall in lake slime.

No. On that day he flew.
The angels came in and
pulled him from the seat
without unfastening his seat belt –
out the back window as if
by magic.

For me, it was magic that the last
activity he did, the last
thing that he did not want
to stop doing was fishing.

It was almost like he was not
ready to say goodbye,
but if he must, he wanted to
give me a hug and let me know:
the fishing line was still intact.

Of Tea Cups and Saucers

My life is china set on a lovely outdoor table
awaiting guests coming to drink tea.
Red flower center pieces catch the design colors,
hand painted years ago on each cup and saucer.

Cloth napkins tented on plates meant for scones
beckon guests while the table linens,
blowing gently in a breeze, are a woman's skirt
covering brown legs.

Before anyone arrives,
I turn the cups
so all the handles point
the same direction.
No one will see the chip in mine.

When everyone arrives,
the table becomes second fiddle
to the conversation.
Yet when they leave,
the guests will always remember
the red flower center pieces,
cloth napkins, and how
the tea cups were all identical.

www.ingramcontent.com/pod-product-compliance
Lightning Source LLC
Chambersburg PA
CBHW031342040426
42443CB00006B/437